Poems from the Pond

Poems from the Pond

Candice Stover

PUBLISHED BY

Deerbrook Editions

P.O. Box 542

Cumberland, Maine 04021-0542

207-829-5038

FIRST EDITION

ISBN: 0-9712488-7-7

On the cover:

At the Pond, pastel by Tom Curry

www.tomcurrymaineartist.com

Cover design and book design by *Jeffrey Haste*

Contents

Introduction   9

Beyond Comparing   13

Intuition   14

The Swim   16

In Lucy's *Boulangerie*   18

Breaking Clouds, Chances in July   19

Briefly, Enough   21

Bedtime Story   22

Summer House   24

Check-out Time at the Rooming House, August   26

Balm   28

Living Where the Sun Still Sets   29

After the Argument   31

February: Leap Year   32

In Season: Five Tankas from the Pond   34

Appointment   36

Acknowledgements   41

There is no language that is not the wording of our habitat, and no self whatever, except a temporary formation of the total environment.

—Robert Aitken

Introduction

"Little jewel," we call it, though of course that's not its real name.

"Let's walk to the pond," we say. And in every season, we do. Sometimes we walk there with skates slung over our shoulders, following our breath to the tilted rock where we lace up and set out to skim the pond's surface. Sometimes we go barefoot, draped in towels, languid in the August heat, heading for an evening swim. We've paddled our canoe across it on crisp fall mornings, watched the ice on it thicken and return—eventually—to air, heard the loons telling it stories in the dark.

Our pond holds a lot of stories. And, like any good storyteller, the pond lives somewhere between stillness and the world of particulars. In the seventeen years it's been our neighbor, the pond is a place we've gone seeking stillness, a place we've entrusted with certain particulars from our own life story just five minutes down the road.

It's the place we watched a small boy release a two-inch baby snapping turtle from a yogurt container into what suddenly looked like an endless body of water. It's the place we skinny-dipped before our wedding day. It's the place we met a survivor from the Holocaust concentration camps—her number tattooed on her forearm—and saw her lean her cane on a stone before slipping into the water to breaststroke under the morning light. It's the place one friend, a biologist, showed me my first snow flea, and another friend, a poet, floated luxuriously there on her back one hot July afternoon, sighing, "It feels like custard!"

It's the place I swam every morning the summer my father was dying and remembered how he carried me on his shoulders, swimming across another Maine body of water when I was a child. I swam almost all the way to the little island in the middle of the pond and back, accompanied by his memory, and emerged somehow feeling lighter, stronger. Then I drove three hours south to the hospital to visit him. The smell of the pond on my skin comforted me.

Who knows how many stories the pond could tell, the memories it has stored and released in the language of raindrops, leaf shadow, wing-beats of the bat, and rising fish in the face of the moon. Even before the first settler of our town, Abraham Somes, moved here in 1761 to make casks and barrels, leaving his name to continue, the pond spoke this language. I like imagining that Somes, too, found comfort and refreshment at the pond; that he, too, felt the gift of its solace.

Mount Desert Island
August 2007

Poems from the Pond

Beyond Comparing

My friend Bear tells me
he likes a challenge. But what
I like is to slip
into the cup of morning,
sip it and not spill one drop.

Intuition

This one, from his first steps, longed
to carry home in his arms all creatures
wild, bovine, other, rare. As if he might
lead the moo-cows he called out to
in the meadow by a string drawn
from his pocket, might guide them
to his bedside and tie them there,
cow by cow, like private angels
to watch a boy sleep.

Once, by a lake, three deer lifted
their heads and watched him approach,
let him take his stance of entrancement
and did not run. The boy turned eight.
That summer his father found a turtle
stranded between ditch and pavement,
a baby snapper he scooped in his palm
to bring home.

The boy kept it in a sink on the porch.
He tempted his turtle with bits of grass,
lumps of hamburger, lettuce, strawberries.
He gave it a rock to stand on, cooled it
with rain trickled from the red spout
of his mother's Mexican watering can.
The black curves of the turtle's tiny claws
strained and scratched to climb the basin.
Its head, a leather thumb, stretched for sky.

Every day the boy nudged the rough puzzle
of its shell and studied the sleepy slits
of its eyes. He named it a secret name.
This went on for a week. Then, one twilight
under a quarter moon, the boy cradled
the turtle into a paper cup and walked
to the pond.

The Swim

I go to him with my skin wrapped
in pond water, the cries of loons
still running wild in my ears, fish
flicking under my kicking toes,
arms spread like wings moving
in moving water.

I go to him reciting names
he taught me for bodies of water
(syllables odd, yet familiar)—
Moosehead and *Kennebec, Saco,
Kezar, Sebago*—the naming
of moving water.

I go to him with the fragrance
of pond lilies slipped through my hair,
eased in every crevice, receptive
as air and reinvented
in my skin by the calm found stroking
in moving water.

I go to him remembering his skin,
his shoulders, the span of his blades
carrying me forward—a child
on her father's back, their bodies
made of summer and advancing
in moving water.

My father the swimmer
my father the fish
the quick fins glistening
and the shore approaching us
here in this other summer.

In Lucy's *Boulangerie*

. . . there are daisies opening
in bouquets she's gathered and striated stones from long walks
up and down all the roads she's lived on.
Strange castings of frogs guard the door.
Paintbrushes stand upright in a glass jar on the Mason
and Hamlin piano, mingling scents of solvent
and warm grain in the air of the unlocked rooms
where Lucy lives. A man has gone, no trace
of his face among the photos of beautiful children
growing up near the counter, where Lucy's hands remember
the intimate rhythm of kneading and turning
the dough, leaving you (on a perfect summer day)
one domed loaf, golden and seeded in the pattern of a star,
delectable pleasure to carry home in your bare hands, still cooling.
Her red swimsuit hangs on the line.

Breaking Clouds, Chances in July

But what could be more ordinary—
                                extraordinary!

The clothes rack draped in white laundry, sky
again discovering blue

after days of mushroom, damp so penetrating
a friend and I lit wood last night

to warm us telling stories full of numbers
(25, 82, 56),

our children and our mothers slipping out of years,
startling us

(as if that summer blouse, swaying on a hanger
in the breeze,

began speaking in a woman's voice, the one
who just yesterday

buttoned it over her breasts)—
the light!

A cloud breaks, sun splashing bees trembling lobes
of honeysuckle

as I sit in wicker reading of another war, grief speechless
as new lettuces leafing

between pea vines twined for sun and a hummingbird
suspending iridescence,

perfectly, over a blossom, when a chestnut buck steps
from the hedge of wild blackberries

to pass, in full view:
                              the white laundry, the empty blouse,

breaking clouds and all that honeysuckle sweetness becoming
one more entry almost missed.

Briefly, Enough

this morning light trembled
through my lashes
as I drifted in   and out
of sleep, cheek resting
on my love's chest

I could follow every breath

a breeze passing over our bodies moved
like another breath, another
kind of breathing, until it seemed
we were drowsing in an open vessel
on a body of water we did not need to name

Bedtime Story

for Peter Sandberg

Once there was a man plunged into dark
when his heart's companion vanished.
He wheeled her, wing and bone, to the bright mouth
of the ambulance on their shady street
and watched her disappear down the avenue
where solitude appeared:
hunk of grief, fist and ache, the hole of all
that was.

Once there was a man following a flatbed
hauling two engraved gravestones
(one his own). He swung into that lane
behind the letters of his name
and saw his birth date by the blank
left for his death, shocked
by completion on the stone beside it.
Where does the beloved go?

(And if he floored the pedal, crashing
into that flatbed scene ahead? *Wow,*
the medic might say, *this guy traveled
prepared.*)

Once there was a man stroking the calm skin
of a pond at dusk, slipping his canoe
among cries of loons, cries
that settled in the throats of lilies, each petal
a vivid piece cut from this first summer

without her. Later, in a cabin built for two,
he pressed a night-light (shaped like a shell)
into the wall, reached through the dark and slept,
like a child, on his own.

Summer House

after a painting by Tom Curry

That long white shadow in the water

but who ever sees a white shadow?

a quickly moving river, full of distortion

but it didn't distort the shadow of the house

the house is a focus, and that crooked splash of spruce

but the house is not the focus, nor the spruce

this painting is about movement

the movement of water and how water is

how water appears on a summer afternoon

not a plain of water, but a wall, rungs climbing

color out of cool depths, the earth soaked, steeped in heat

can you feel the river slipping past reflection?

summer   its vivid opposites   light passing through

that blue wall of the summer house, facing back—

24

doesn't the house look as if it, too, might be made of water?

Check-out Time at the Rooming House, August

Some of you will want to know who stayed here
and what it felt like, sleeping in the corner room
with a breeze, the fan making its cool back talk
to one wedged in the kitchen window opposite.

Downstairs we could hear someone snoring,
plowing the tunnels of bliss in animal slumber,
while upstairs Roni from Israel defended war
forking tuna fish out of a can.

(*God*, Kevin said the next morning, *that was intense.*)

Giggles next door undressed Angie and Dan
as new lovers (we'd seen her tattoo, a violet sun
rising between cappuccino shoulder blades, heard
his sound system, wired with sighs and murmurs).

(*God,* Kevin said the next morning, *that was intense.*)

And because Bob, our innkeeper, also had mentioned
a two-year-old (*Babies*, he said, *are a fact of life*), then
told us of one packed in a saddlebag, riding horseback
to Stowe, Massachusetts in 1898, how could a half-pint

named Carter surprise us the next morning, emerging
from the room at the end of the hall and heading
straight for Kevin's hairy knees by the pot-bellied stove
and a society of suitcases assembled for departure,

chiming his new favorite word:

Go! Go! Go!

Balm

After the reunion's excess
of company and champagne,

just the two of us ease
the canoe into the pond.

September's leaves light lamps
around us; we paddle

into gold suffusion as if
entering a ripe pear.

Our blades low, we lean
and listen—the surface insects

hectic, the cool still depths.
A pair of wood ducks squawks

away. The fruity air softens,
darkening, as one by one

the reeds extend themselves
exactly by reflection.

Living Where the Sun Still Sets

Once again the rim
of the earth is burning.
Clouds smolder then dark
begins, draping privacy
over every shape it finds here:
                        colony of boulders
in a field, tangle of oaks,
houses and machinery.

Even the leaves disappear.

Eleven thousand miles south,
not one leaf: only ice
and the history of ice
holding its own
in a season where the sun doesn't set.

But here the pond has slipped
beneath a darker glisten.
Our neighbor's windows shine.
I drop the blinds and turn back
to those pages recording
Shackleton's last expedition:
                        frost-smoke, pacing
and Worsley taking observations
of the sun whenever possible . . .
on the march for a week, fearing
sunstroke even at two a.m. and then . . .

> . . . *no alternative*
> (Shackleton writes) *but to camp*
> *once more on the ice floe*
> *and to possess our souls*
> *with what patience we could* . . .

The slow drift to evening
at another latitude . . .

After the Argument

Between sharp words and a silence,
the night swim:
the two of us stepping off the roof
down the ladder
to the brick walk bordered by nasturtiums
and lettuces, cool
flounce of headed leaves between spicy blossoms
you can eat
(we'd picked some for a salad, afterwards);

but first things
first (even if we do them last),
as we do
tonight, entering the water in the almost dark,
our bodies breaking
into what feels like liquid silk, invisible hum and arc
of everything living
on and off and under the pond's surface, creatures
of blood, here like us,

being fed, being soothed.

February: Leap Year

For two days

       and two nights,

              snow falls.

Near twilight

       on the second day,

              we step

onto our skis

       to break trail

              across the pond.

We glide through

       snow, a wall

              of feathers

at our feet.

       White flakes fall

              swiftly

from black sky.

       Our skis hiss

              and sift

as we make tracks

       towards illusions

              of horizon.

White lines meet

        converge

              disappear.

In Season: Five Tankas from the Pond

1. April Thaw
for Jane Disney

Thinnest near the edge,
white layers keep vanishing: breath
over dark water.
Sublimation, science calls
it, how we change forms, hover . . .

2. Latitude: Coyotes in Winter

Shrill city yanking
its twilight chain, unleashing
what still clamors, wild
to reach us, touching what's raw—
Dusk sinks the pond plum.

3. Waking After Midnight: That Thirst

One loon calling, one
note floating from the pond's dark
kingdom   bats gliding
blind   mosquitoes whine, sucking
blood   leaves sizzle   wings beat   hush

4. On a Day She Heard No Voices

The pond: tea-colored
dark clarities   no memory
of ice sealing it
then—shearing up—gradually
she enters her reflection

5. Minus 14 Degrees Fahrenheit, with Wind-chill

Ice like a bandit
steals the pond overnight, shuts
fragile edges in
where clouds float lilac, early
sunset: cold jewels burning

Appointment

Not that it knows my name
or that I call it
any name at all—

pond, refuge, sanity, little jewel . . .

Not that it knows I approach it
summer mornings
like a lover

I undress for without hesitating—
sandals on the bank,
towel draping the branches,

welcoming even the sharp stones
it passes over
like certain betrayals . . .

how I lie on my side and let
the cool of its skin
brush my cheek, float

my body, this surface
where the loon also learns
how to cry for its species

and where stems of bladderwort rise
above the ugliness
of our name for it:

those delicate carnivores
I am not afraid to swim near
with their beautiful open mouths.

Acknowledgements

Acknowledgements are due to the editors of the following publications, in whose pages some of the poems in this book first appeared.

The essay in the introduction appeared in *Maine Voices: a Celebration of the People of Maine and the Places They Love*, as part of Stories from the Maine Voices Project published by the Wilderness Society in 2004.

Intuition appeared in **Friends of Acadia Journal**.

Summer House was part of a collaboration with the painter Tom Curry for the 2nd Annual Belfast Poetry Presentation in October 2006.

February: Leap Year originally appeared in **Holding Patterns** (Muse Press), selected by Mary Oliver for the Maine Chapbook Award 1994.

A selection of the tankas appeared in *Writing Nature*.

With thanks to Kate Barnes, Kathleen Ellis, Kristen Lindquist, and Elizabeth Tibbetts for their attention through the years to poems in progress.

Thanks to my husband, Jeff Toman, for bringing me to the pond and continuing to share the elements.

Candice Stover is a native of Maine who has traveled and taught widely, including two years in Shanghai, China and workshops in New Zealand. A former reporter for *The Boston Globe*, she is the author of two poetry collections, *Holding Patterns* (Muse Press), selected by Mary Oliver for a Maine Chapbook Award, and *Another Stopping Place* (Oyster River Press), as well as appearing in the anthology, *The Other Side of Sorrow: Poets Speak Out about Conflict, War, and Peace*, and a variety of journals and magazines. She lives on Mount Desert Island, where she teaches at College of the Atlantic, designs and facilitates independent writing workshops, and swims in or bicycles by or walks to Somes Pond almost every day.